Young

WONDER VERSE

A Canvas Of Words

Edited By Lynsey Evans

First published in Great Britain in 2025 by:

Young Writers
Remus House
Coltsfoot Drive
Peterborough
PE2 9BF
Telephone: 01733 890066
Website: www.youngwriters.co.uk

Book Design by Ashley Janson

Softback ISBN 978-1-83685-224-7
Printed and bound in the UK by BookPrintingUK
Website: www.bookprintinguk.com
YB0628B

FOREWORD

WELCOME READER,

For Young Writers' latest competition *Wonderverse*, we asked primary school pupils to explore their creativity and write a poem on any topic that inspired them. They rose to the challenge magnificently with some going even further and writing stories too! The result is this fantastic collection of writing in a variety of styles.

Here at Young Writers our aim is to encourage creativity in children and to inspire a love of the written word, so it's great to get such an amazing response, with some absolutely fantastic pieces. This open theme of this competition allowed them to write freely about something they are interested in, which we know helps to engage kids and get them writing. Within these pages you'll find a variety of topics, from hopes, fears and dreams, to favourite things and worlds of imagination. The result is a collection of brilliant writing that showcases the creativity and writing ability of the next generation.

I'd like to congratulate all the young writers in this anthology, I hope this inspires them to continue with their creative writing.

CONTENTS

Ashley Academy, South Shields

Ethan Mukuruva (10) 1
Isaac Reah (9) 2
Eva Swinbanks (9) 4
Bobbi Price (10) 5
Isabel Marie Bates (10) 6

Burrelton Primary School, Burrelton

Isabella Boyd (9) 7
Rachel Elizabeth May Binnie (11) 8
Ava Frost (11) 10
Olivia Taylor (10) 11
Ella Falconer 12
Ria Levens (11) 13
Emily White (10) 14

Clarborough Primary School, Clarborough

Joe Hitchcock (8) 15
Isabella Poulton (8) 16
Rosie Baker (9) 17
Alana Scott (9) 18
Annabelle Hoult (8) 19
Emily Smith (8) 20

Hatton Park Primary School, Longstanton

Aoife Horne (8) 21
Harry Dawson (8) 22
Akira Reddy (8) 23
Sam O'Neill (9) 24

John Ball Primary School, Blackheath

Elin Wigfall (9) 25
Sahana Chase (10) 26
Lucy Knight (8) 28
Phoebe Ayres (9) 29
Dollie Mahoney (10) 30
Pearl Davies (9) 31
Viktoria Beierlein (10) 32
Hayden Amias Buckley (10) 33
Hezekiah Quartey-Atror (9) 34
Adina Balogun (11) 35
Maye Esimaje (10) 36
Sienna Bois-Pursey (11) 37
Afsah Kamran (9) 38
Maya Tropia Thwaites (9) 39
Tommy Lynam 40
Carina Scott (8) 41
Zoe Abram (7) 42
Orson Mahoney (7) 43
Penny Moyle (9) 44
Lailah Allyson Prager Castro (11) 45
Ramona Bello-Torres (8) 46
Frida Leung (7) 47
Vera Kontchakov (8) 48
Chloe Reed (7) 49
Kalina Olechowska (8) 50
Alicja Wojda (7) 51
Josh Chiu (8) 52
Sophia Taylor (7) 53
Joshua Mandlik-Smith (7) 54
Harley Dyer (7) 55
Mariia Zhozhina (9) 56
Raymi May Queija Harris (8) 57
Lucian Rothlisberger (10) 58

Mia Ratto-Olsen (7) 59
Roman Zoller (7) 60

Kentmere Academy And Nursery, Rochdale

Oduwa Evbuomwan (9) 61
Esta-Mae Hodgson (9) 62
Lavinia Rosca (9) 64
Ibrahim Martaza (9) 65
Kashif Hussain (9) 66
Peggy Jones (9) 67
Ekamnoor Singh (9) 68
Musa Musaib (10) 69
Saad Khalid (9) 70
Dawud Raza (9) 71

Kidmore End CE Primary School, Kidmore End

Oscar Donlon (8) 72

Our Lady & St Joseph RC Primary School, Hackney

Princess Mary Tazi Nsambu (9) 73
Sophia St Louis (9) 74
Narabi Vera Ilumoka (10) 76
Annalise Campbell (9) 78
Eliott Arnoux (9) 79
Elijah McKenzie (10) 80
Geralda Maria (9) 81
Ava Slaymaker 82
Haviliah Ojarikre (9) 83
Luca Grossi (9) 84
Ivy Neave (9) 85
Niamh Buck (10) 86
Aleks Leszkowicz (9) 87
Lois Dunn (9) 88
Anya Piwowarek (9) 89

Priors Field Primary School, Kenilworth

Niamh Allen (11) 90
Niamh R (10) 91
Toby Shute (8) 92
Jess B (10) 93
Penny B (9) 94
Charlotte Williams (9) 95
Joseph Ballinger (9) 96
Winnie CW (8) 97
Evie Whiter (7) 98
Mabel Folliot (9) 99
Maysa Ma (8) 100

St Anne's CE Primary School, Godmanchester

Jack Hopstein (8) 101
James Cashman (8) 102
Jilord Churchill (8) 103
Nina Zolnowska (8) 104
Freddie Mews (9) 105
Caden Outridge 106
Harrison Bishop (8) 107
Autumn Shortt (9) 108
Aoife Yetton (8) 109
Gloria Leacock (8) 110
Ava Stoehr (8) 111
Edward Risley-Settle (8) 112
Jeremiah Smith (9) 113
Mufaro Precious Nyakuedzwa (8) 114
Sienna Price (9) 115
Leonardo Wright (8) 116
Lilah Pennington (9) 117
Oscar Hooper (8) 118
Thomas Hepworth (8) 119
Fynn Rowland (8) 120
Hartley Jackson (8) 121
Samantha Ogeh (8) 122
Millie Gilbert (8) 123
Alexander Akinyele (8) 124
Nora Webb (9) 125
Hayden Warren-Rea (8) 126

St Monica's RC Primary School, Flixton

Sofia Jackson (9)	127
Emilia Attwood (9)	128
Yasmin McKenna (7)	130
Mikey Gallager (8)	131
Michael Nesbitt (8)	132
Jasmine Smith (7)	133
Aibhlinn Maguire (7)	134
Jessica Kelly (7)	135
Ifechi Etolue (8)	136
Emily Morris (7)	137
Fionn Whiting (7)	138
Penny Petrou (9)	139
Madeline Yuille (8)	140
Caleb Fitzgerald (7)	141
Ivy Whitworth (8)	142
Ava Whitworth (7)	143
Evelina Dorling (10)	144

Stoneyburn Primary School, Bathgate

Abbi Condie (9)	145
Ava Lee (10)	146
Lori Bryce (9)	147
Hollie Moore (8)	148
Leah O'Malley (10)	149
Chloe Gilfether (10)	150
Cora Pacey (9)	151

Stopsley High School, Luton

Aroush Fatima Qasim (11)	152

Terrington CE (VA) Primary School, Terrington

Milly Stoker (10)	153
Bea Tyreman (9)	154
Poppy Pesterfeild (10)	155
Matthew Whitcher (10)	156
Isabella Sharp (10)	157

Werrington Community Primary School, Yeolmbridge

Sasha Sefton (9)	158

Whitchurch Primary School, Whitchurch

Edie Short (9)	159
Daisy Howell (10)	160
Cole Preen (10)	161
Nell Smith (9)	162
Chloe Page (9)	163
Leo Edwards	164
Eloise Latham (9)	165
Hollie Williams (9)	166
Gabija Ciunelis (10)	167
Thomas Webley (9)	168
Charlie Young (9)	169
Vinny Skinner (9)	170
Chantai Joseph (9)	171
Emily Alexander (9)	172
Amelia Reeves (10)	173
Scarlett Hill (10)	174
Lawson-John Mullins-Rothwell (10)	175
Isabella Britton (9)	176
Esme Greenan (9)	177
Sophie Tovey (10)	178
Lily James (9)	179
Finley Knight (9)	180
Moyra Mitkova (9)	181

Wilbraham Primary School, Fallowfield

Margot Mansfield Steinhäuser (10)	182
India Rose Denny (10)	184
Jumana Jabir (10)	185
Rayana Albadawi (10)	186
Olah Ahmed (10)	187

Ysgol Gynradd Gymunedol Gymraeg Llantrisant, Miskin

Violet Sheehy (10) 188
Gwion Davies (11) 189

THE
CREATIVE
WRITING
GO
1035

Blue Phoenix

This sun I don't want to stare at,
Reminds me of the Blue Phoenix,
His super strength and fighting skills are great in combat.

Once, a young girl was smacked,
By the evil wizard,
A place dark and hard to find.

Blue Phoenix, fast as lightning,
Came to the rescue,
X-ray vision and super speed,
Can't even predict his next move.

Immortal hero!
The crowd sing,
Safe at last in her mother's arms,
Who can outsmart the people's hero?
Blue Phoenix, a hero in many dimensions.

Ethan Mukuruva (10)
Ashley Academy, South Shields

Friendship

I have many friends
I like to see,
I hope they feel
The same about me.

When we are at school,
We work very hard,
Then at break time,
We play together in the yard.

We learn and play,
For most of the day,
To leave and go home,
At the end of the day.

My friends make me smile,
In the six weeks,
I won't see them,
For a while.

You make me laugh,
And do silly things,
We like to play football,
And play on the swings.

In summer we go
To the beach and fair,
Finding friends like you
Is very rare.

A message to my friends,
For being so great,
I love you all,
Thanks for being my mates.

Isaac Reah (9)
Ashley Academy, South Shields

Spectacular Space

Oh! What an atmosphere,
Way up where skies are clear.
I love shining stars where they're enough above the clouds.
Oh my! Oh my! Crying planets.
Oh no! Oh no!
The moon says, "It's okay, Planets,
No need to cry, for I can sing you a lullaby."
Sun listens in and thinks, *oh wow!*
And winks goodnight.

Eva Swinbanks (9)
Ashley Academy, South Shields

Dreams

Hold on to your dreams, in case they may die
Or fly away to another world, a world that is alone for no one to enter
That can cause you to fade and go to the underworld
Where dreams have been given up on
And no one pays attention to
Dreams that die.

Bobbi Price (10)
Ashley Academy, South Shields

The Meaning Of Friendship

F orever
R eally loyal
I nsane
E xciting adventures
N ot fake
D on't let down
S oulmates
H eaps of fun
I nseparable
P erfect for me.

Isabel Marie Bates (10)
Ashley Academy, South Shields

Halloween

Halloween is spooky and scary with monsters that roam the streets,
Looking for sweet treats to eat.
But don't be alarmed if you hear a knock on the door
On Halloween night. They're probably looking for chocolates and sweets galore.
To fill their buckets and bags to the brim,
And leave your house with a grin.
So I hope you now know what to do,
When you hear a knock at the door,
Bring some sweets and say hello.

Isabella Boyd (9)
Burrelton Primary School, Burrelton

Nothing Lasts Forever

It is now winter, in with the cold,
Let's head outside with the shovel I hold.

With a great big heave and the snow that I rake,
It shall be a snowman that I make,

A few minutes later there were two balls of snow,
With pebbles on the face and a carrot I know,

And with a frightening jolt the snowman bolted awake!
The boy was shocked (he thought he was fake!),

"Don't worry. I'm not that scary!" the snowman said.
Then the boy laughed so hard he almost lost his head!

From that day on the boy saw him every day,
They fit perfectly like a fish and the River Tay!

They talked all day until the boy was told,
To get inside before his dinner went cold!

It is now spring and the boy's out for his snowman
And it is freakishly hot he almost had a suntan!

But little did the boy know,
That there would be no snow,

He ran right over to come and say, "Hey!"
But he saw the carrot and pebbles in a puddle that day,

The boy fell to his knees to help his friend,
But then realised it wasn't an easy mend,

The boy couldn't help it, he began to cry,
Until he noticed the red in his eye,

But then he realised, "Nothing lasts forever."
And after all that they're still together.

Rachel Elizabeth May Binnie (11)
Burrelton Primary School, Burrelton

What Am I?

As old as time, can you figure out my rhyme?
I have one pair of wings,
A fire in me,
You wouldn't want to see,
I'm in the air,
Without a care.

I have thousands of gold,
In a hold in my lair,
I have no hair.

If anyone comes in,
They won't come out,
What am I?

Answer: A dragon.

Ava Frost (11)
Burrelton Primary School, Burrelton

Besties

B eautifully laughing along,
E ncouraging,
S afe together forever,
T rusting each other.

F riendly, giving hugs,
R especting each other,
I ncluded always,
E lated together,
N ourishing words of kindness,
D aydreaming together,
S uper supportive.

Olivia Taylor (10)
Burrelton Primary School, Burrelton

Summer

S un shining beautifully in the blue, cloudy sky
U mbrella is not being needed
M ango drinks being sipped by the chilly pool
M oving around, playing with best friends
E veryone having a great time
R eady to go to the shining, sunny beach.

Ella Falconer
Burrelton Primary School, Burrelton

What Season Am I?

In Scotland,
I am every weather,
Such as a pinch of cold and torrential rain,
It is such a beautiful time of year,
Such lovely leaves,
Such elation for the animals,
Time to eat and wake up,
Of course, the answer is Spring!

Ria Levens (11)
Burrelton Primary School, Burrelton

Calves

C an't you see them over the hill?
A ll of them, every single one.
L ike them munching on tasty grass.
V ery cute calves.
E veryone loves calves.
S ome calves have beautiful spots.

Emily White (10)
Burrelton Primary School, Burrelton

Winter

Cold, frosty mornings,
Cobwebs sparkle like glitter,
Crunching footsteps on the icy grass,
Smashing up ice in puddles.

Bare trees looking like finger bones,
Reaching out in the cold mist,
Frozen breath like a dragon breathing,
Tingling fingers frozen with cold.

Dancing snowflakes everywhere,
Turning and tumbling to the ground,
Children playing and making snowmen,
Snowball fights all around.

Home to cosy winter fires,
Children hanging up stockings on Christmas Eve,
Excitedly waiting in their beds
For Father Christmas to fill them.

Joe Hitchcock (8)
Clarborough Primary School, Clarborough

Animals

Dogs and frogs, and big fat hogs,
Cats and rats, and scary bats,
Lions and tigers, and big brown bears,
From whales that are the size of a bus,
To insects that don't make a fuss,
There are animals in our world,
But this is a planet we must share,
To love and protect, and help and care.
So stand up now, get off your phone,
Or we'll live in this world all alone,
So just you listen to my words,
A planet without dogs and cats, and birds,
Will be a terrible place, of course,
Without my favourite...

A chestnut horse.

Isabella Poulton (8)
Clarborough Primary School, Clarborough

Nature's Love

Splash goes the water in the emerald-green forest.
You can hear the leaves rustling in the slow breeze
As the creature appears, its paws crunching through the grass
And sits on a soft patch of moss.
Then, out of nowhere, there is a thundering...
Bang echoing and the creature thumps with a loud bash
When its paws reach the ground
And the creature's family come out.
And they snuggle and purr
It is calm and quiet
You can still hear the slashing
And the rustling
That place is the place to be.

Rosie Baker (9)
Clarborough Primary School, Clarborough

The Pumpkin

Yellow, white or green they're all the same you see,
A bit like dot to dot.
Don't be afraid, they're only for decoration,
But sometimes they can live up to your expectations.
Don't worry it won't go to waste,
You can make pumpkin pie with the waste.
It's orange and crusty and it's super creamy,
I'm sure you will like it too.
And maybe if you have a sweet tooth,
Some whipped cream too!
And if you want to have the best pumpkin,
You can put candy in it too.

Alana Scott (9)
Clarborough Primary School, Clarborough

Just One Wish

I have
Just one wish
To be like Peter Pan
And never grow up

You try hard
To catch your shadow
But it moves too fast

So come with me
Where dreams are born
Because once you're grown up
You can't come back
To your childhood

People always ask me
What I want to be when I grow up
Well, I have just one wish
To never grow up, never grow up, never grow up.

Annabelle Hoult (8)
Clarborough Primary School, Clarborough

All About A Mischievous Fox

Hi, I am Emily. I love foxes. They scream loudly like a dog barking. One night, I was walking home, and I saw a lonely fox crying in the forest in the dark. At first, I wanted to hug it, but I knew it would scamper off, so I left it alone and after a day, I saw it and now it was nowhere but in my house, so I adopted it, and now it lives in a cot at the end of the store.
Bye-bye.

Emily Smith (8)
Clarborough Primary School, Clarborough

Thunder, Thunder In The Sky

Thunder, thunder in the sky,
Makes some people cry,
But I think that's a lie.

It rumbles and rumbles,
And rumbles on,
To me it sounds,
A bit like a song.

Through the clouds,
You can also see,
A bit of lightning,
For you and for me.

In my car,
Listening to the rain.
Rata-tat-tat, it goes,
Down the drain.

Once the big storm has passed,
The thunder is finally gone at last.

Aoife Horne (8)
Hatton Park Primary School, Longstanton

Dino Roar

D eadly Dilophosaurus spits venom
I nvented Indominus Rex was man-made
N ippy Nanshiungosaurus, the speediest sprinter of its time
O mnivorous Oviraptor ate meat, eggs and seeds
S pine-chilling Spinosaurus taller and longer than a T-rex
A ngry Ankylosaurus thrashes its tail
U ndecided if the Utahraptor had feathers
R oar! Roar! Roar!

Harry Dawson (8)
Hatton Park Primary School, Longstanton

Autumn

Harvest Festival comes around,
Bushes of blackberries can be found.
For some, the school days have begun,
The summer holidays have been and gone.
September and October, bring darker nights,
A warmer coat to wrap up tight.
The insets now seem far and few,
The trees grow bare, a sky less blue.
First came spring, then summer sun,
Now the autumn has begun.

Akira Reddy (8)
Hatton Park Primary School, Longstanton

Summer

S ummer is fun
U nder the sun
M aple tree
M aple tree all aglow
E veryone's thrilled
R ushing around, at the den build.

Sam O'Neill (9)
Hatton Park Primary School, Longstanton

I Don't Like My Stuff

I don't like my hat,
It's frilly, smells like a lily,
And looks like a cat,
That's why I don't like my hat.

I don't like my pet,
It's got a stupid name, it's super lame
And I won it in a bet,
That's why I don't like my pet.

I don't like my wig,
It's curly and hurly-burly
And smells like a pig
That's why I don't like my wig.

I don't like my pyjamas,
They are super tight, the colours are bright
And the patterns are llamas,
That's why I don't like my pyjamas.

I don't like my stuff,
My hat, my pet, my wig, my pyjamas, everything!
And that's that.
I hate my stuff and my stuff hates me!

Elin Wigfall (9)
John Ball Primary School, Blackheath

The Most Important Thing

Friends are the most important thing,
They will be there for you when times are tough.
Whether you've had a bereavement or are simply lost,
They will always be there to guide you.
They'll reach out their hand when you are drowning,
Helping you up until you've found your feet again.
You can share anything with them,
They will listen.
You will make memories and share the good times and bad together,
And will achieve impossible things together,
Because nothing is impossible if you have a friend.
Your imagination and creativity will grow,
You will together go from seeds to blossoming, thriving trees.
But what's this?
A little creature is nipping at your bond...
This creature is nibbling your thread of friendship!
Suddenly, the thread of friendship turns from calm green to amber,
You and your friend then start fussing and arguing.
The pesky creature continues to nibble at your thread of friendship.
Soon, your thread of friendship turns a furious red.

You and your friend start to slip away from each other,
Slowly falling, falling, falling...
But no, you will not give up.
An argument will not stop you from achieving your dreams together.
You are brave, strong and courageous.
You never give up.
So you and your friend lunge at this vile creature,
Sending it scuttling away.
Slowly, your thread of friendship turns back to its peaceful green.
You and your friend held on,
Never giving up,
And when you don't give up,
Amazing things will happen.
And guess what?
Those two went on to achieve their impossible dreams together,
And went on to have many great adventures because they never gave up.
And guess what?
If you never stop trying and never stop believing,
You will achieve your dreams someday,
Because you have a friend,
And friends are the most important thing.

Sahana Chase (10)
John Ball Primary School, Blackheath

Upstairs

I never go upstairs,
There's a 'thing' upstairs,
And when I lie in bed at night,
I hear it jumping side to side,
Like it's playing hopscotch,
But it isn't very good.

When I lie in bed at night,
I think I smell damp earth,
Like the corner of the playground,
Full of possibilities.

When I lie in bed at night,
I see shadows on my wall,
That grow and move and change,
Reminding me of things I've seen.

I never go upstairs,
There's a 'thing' upstairs,
I feel it might be just like me - I'm going upstairs.

Lucy Knight (8)
John Ball Primary School, Blackheath

Lazy

I never do anything.
I never paint.
I never play.

I just do nothing.
But then I'm ordered to do my homework.
So, I find a pencil and I find myself doodling.
So, I get a paintbrush and paint.
I open my never-used set of watercolours
And paint a rainbow.
I make a collage and colour my rainbow.
I go outside and play in the rain
I get soaked and I can feel my leggings
Seeping water to my legs and drowning my feet.
But I don't care because I've got a lot of energy.
I never stop.
I never give up
Because I am super.

Phoebe Ayres (9)
John Ball Primary School, Blackheath

What Am I?

This is a poem about what I am,
I am grey like the night sky,
I howl in the dark and I sneak around in the daylight,
I sometimes live in a cave,
But sometimes I live in woodlands,
For dinner, I eat deer and for breakfast, I eat moose,
I come from Eurasia,
I produce pups,
And once again, can you guess what I am?
And if you guessed correctly, this was your answer,
A scary wolf,
A creepy wolf,
A wolf that only lives at night,
Or just a wolf,
A wolf can be anything you want,
A dark wolf,
A scary wolf,
A fluffy wolf.

Dollie Mahoney (10)
John Ball Primary School, Blackheath

Life Is Everything

Life is worth more than gold
No one can replace you, you are you, no matter what
Your personality is worth more than all the pearls in the deep blue sea
Because you can be you and I can be me
Life is worth everything, more than the jewels of the king
Even if you want to disagree, everything is momentary, even if it's not clear
Because life is not replaceable, even if you believe in Heaven
You can't jump off a mountain just because you think of lucky number seven!
So the message that you can see
Is nothing is worth more than you and me!

Pearl Davies (9)
John Ball Primary School, Blackheath

War

Bullets coming down as fast rain
The sky was so gloomy it felt unreal
Imagine what those brave soldiers felt having a bullet across their heart, that would be painful.
Soldiers falling down not able to feel their limbs and not able to stand up on their own on two feet like a seal.
War is a raging beast
Clashing swords hitting swiftly
The tension expanding like what yeast does to flour.
Some people with pity,
War is not good but peace is.
Peace is good but war isn't.

Viktoria Beierlein (10)
John Ball Primary School, Blackheath

Peace Versus War

Peace is broken,
War wreaks out in havoc,
Like a broken hammock,
Does war have to be this cruel?
Can't it just be very small?

Peace is bittersweet,
War is sweetly bitter.
Does war have to be mean?
Can't it just be as quick as a stream?

Rain is lead bullets falling from the sky,
It's the opposite of a butterfly.
But peace is stronger than war.
We can stop war!

Hayden Amias Buckley (10)
John Ball Primary School, Blackheath

My Adventure Out Into Space

Across the stars, above the sea,
I see a world like you and me,
Where galaxies stretch endlessly,
With echoes drifting from a mystery place.

Bright lights coming from afar,
Each a twinkling star,
Reminding me of infinite possibilities,
What else do I see?

I travel through a cosmic sky,
Then I wonder, who am I?
I am sorry, my friends, I have to go,
I shall see you in the snow.

Hezekiah Quartey-Atror (9)
John Ball Primary School, Blackheath

Don't Cry

Don't cry when the rain falls upon you,
Don't cry when friendships die,
It's okay to ask for help.

Don't cry if the sun won't shine,
You shine.

If you think there is no way out,
Don't cry.
Be strong, stay strong and feel strong.

Don't cry because the plants won't grow.
Don't cry because your feelings won't show.
Don't cry.

Adina Balogun (11)
John Ball Primary School, Blackheath

War And Peace

War and peace,
We can set war free off its lead,
Or we can capture it once and release
Peace.

War and peace,
To have peace is to love,
To love is to have peace, learn to love it.
Embrace it.
Peace.

War and peace,
War is like a hail storm drifting down the streets.
War is the enemy of speech.
Don't embrace it.

War.
War and peace.

Maye Esimaje (10)
John Ball Primary School, Blackheath

Peace

Peace is what some want and others do not,
But unfortunately, war is here and there.
Okay, just let me tell you, people get hurt,
Even if that person is so annoying that you hurt them,
How would you feel if you were that person getting hurt?
Even if their name is next.
Peace is soft music,
So even if you are hurt,
Don't hurt others,
Treat others how you want to be treated.

Sienna Bois-Pursey (11)
John Ball Primary School, Blackheath

Cultures

Karachi is in Pakistan,
Tokyo is in Japan,
Cairo is in Egypt,
New York is in the United States,
Bogotá is in Colombia,
London is in England,
Madrid is in Spain,
Venice is in Italy,
Paris is in France,
Sydney is in Australia.
Wherever you are,
Whoever you are,
We all embrace different cultures,
Like the Irish,
Like the Italians.

Afsah Kamran (9)
John Ball Primary School, Blackheath

Colours

Red
Blood is red, roses are red, so is my bed
Blue
The ocean is blue, the sky is too
Green
The grass is green and runner beans
Yellow
The sun is yellow and the meadows
White
The snow is white and so is bright light
Grey
Dolphins are grey and so is today
Brown
Bears are brown and so is my dressing gown
My world is colours.

Maya Tropia Thwaites (9)
John Ball Primary School, Blackheath

Ahmet

Ahmet the Syrian refugee,
Walked up mountains and climbed some trees.
But when he crossed the giant sea,
Sadly his sister had to flee.
Then he went to the country of Greece.

And walked across Europe like ghee,
And finally went to Germany.
And lived a life of harmony,
Until he got stung by a bee.
At the ripe old age of 93.

Tommy Lynam
John Ball Primary School, Blackheath

Adorable Dog

Adorable dog,
I love the way,
You point your paw,
"That way!" you say.

"Let's find a game to play all day!"

That way you woof,
That way you call,
My heart starts bouncing,
Like a ball.

You race across the fields so fast,
Lightning bolting through the grass!

I want to take you home with me,
So you can be my family.
Adorable dog...

Carina Scott (8)
John Ball Primary School, Blackheath

Tadpoles

T errific tadpoles all around,
A dorable creatures to be about,
D ancing in the swamp, just not gonna stop!
P eaceful creatures, so nice and calm,
O nly the one you can count on,
L eaving a trail of water behind them,
E ating seaweed to become a frog,
S o much fun!

Zoe Abram (7)
John Ball Primary School, Blackheath

Robot In The World Of Space

There once was a robot called Beep Bop
He travelled in a rocket called Pop
He went into outer space
Where he found bones of the human race.

The planet's name was Lersaze
It was once attacked by asteroid rains
Inside the asteroids were crystals producing black mist
Which filled the humans with bliss.

Orson Mahoney (7)
John Ball Primary School, Blackheath

Snake

Shimmering in the pale moonlight
Kills another with just a bite
Limbless, scaly, invisible to sight
Smoothly slithering
Uncloaks its veil
Continues on its treacherous trail
Sleek and shiny
Glowing tail
Multicoloured
Against the gale
A monster, a legend
A myth, a mystery
A snake!

Penny Moyle (9)
John Ball Primary School, Blackheath

Peace

Peace is in everybody's heart,
Peace is the opposite of war,
Peace is like when you're warm and cosy in the cold,
Peace is why everybody's kind,
Peace is a breeze in your dream when you sleep,
Peace is love,
Peace is hope,
Peace is calm,
Peace will start to be the world.

Lailah Allyson Prager Castro (11)
John Ball Primary School, Blackheath

Guinea Pigs Rule

Guinea pigs rule
Even though they never went to school
So they're really, really cool!
They help you get to school
Because they know it's the only way you'll rule
And if you don't, you'd be a fool.
So everyone, don't be dumb
Get a guinea pig and join in the fun!

Ramona Bello-Torres (8)
John Ball Primary School, Blackheath

Under The Waterfall

Under the waterfall lies a secret cavern
In the secret cavern lies a never-ending pile of silver
In the never-ending pile of silver lies a secret box
In the secret box lies a secret egg
Who knows what lies in the secret egg
Maybe you know, but it remains a mystery for now.

Frida Leung (7)
John Ball Primary School, Blackheath

Frog Friend

Once I had a frog
Who jumped on a log
In a very green bog
And started singing

I said, "My dear frog,
A witch called Mog
Who lives at the same bog
Is inviting us for tea."

After that we had a nice long walk
And a very interesting talk
With my funny friend frog
And a cup of hot tea.

Vera Kontchakov (8)
John Ball Primary School, Blackheath

Sea Life

S wimming with the animals.
E njoying swimming with the fish.
A nimals in the sea are great.

L ife with the fish.
I magine you're a mermaid.
F loating in the ocean.
E njoy the aquarium.

Chloe Reed (7)
John Ball Primary School, Blackheath

On The Way Home In October

Burning red leaves, swishing as the wind blows,
Like mini bonfires shining in the air,
Some of them golden, like medals on the trees,
We watch the sunset in admiration,
As it sends rays of light through,
The low clouds over the heath.

Kalina Olechowska (8)
John Ball Primary School, Blackheath

My Magical House

My magical house is on top of a tree with purple leaves. My magical house is made of branches and rocks and inside is a portal to another world called Animal Realm. It's a realm where hedgehogs are pink and squirrels are blue and trees are yellow.

Alicja Wojda (7)
John Ball Primary School, Blackheath

Coco In Bed

When I looked at Coco in her bed,
All I could see was a dog waiting to be fed.
My mum came in with a bag of food,
But surprisingly she was in a bad mood.
Staring at the meat she likes to eat,
She suddenly jumped to her feet.

Josh Chiu (8)
John Ball Primary School, Blackheath

Halloween

H appy Halloween
A argh!
L ots of laughs
L aughs and liquorice
O range ogres
W hite werewolves
E erie evening
E nticing eats
N ight night.

Sophia Taylor (7)
John Ball Primary School, Blackheath

What's Your Favourite?

What's your favourite food?
Is it a kebab?
What's your favourite name?
Is it Gabe?
What's your favourite transport?
Is it a bike?
What's your favourite hobby?
Is it to hike?

Joshua Mandlik-Smith (7)
John Ball Primary School, Blackheath

Emotions

Sometimes, I'm sad.
Sometimes, I'm mad.
Sometimes, I'm happy.
Sometimes, I'm chatty.

But all the feelings I've had.
Don't make me sad.
They make me glad.

Harley Dyer (7)
John Ball Primary School, Blackheath

Magician

One night on dream line,
A guy said he might turn me into a pine,
Because I screamed about him in bed,
And didn't get red,
It turned out he was a magician,
Who hated addition.

Mariia Zhozhina (9)
John Ball Primary School, Blackheath

Tree

T reating people so they're able to live,
R eciting poetry under the tree to give,
E nriching giver of air to breathe,
E ternal sustainer of humanity.

Raymi May Queija Harris (8)
John Ball Primary School, Blackheath

Gods Do Whaaat?

Hermes pinches Athena's nose
Apollo rhymes
Dionysus whines
Poseidon waves
Zeus bolts.

Lucian Rothlisberger (10)
John Ball Primary School, Blackheath

Why Do I Love Pandas?

Why do I love pandas?
Bamboo with lavender.
Why do I love flowers?
Grass with showers.

Mia Ratto-Olsen (7)
John Ball Primary School, Blackheath

Summer

A haiku

Summer has ditched us
Walking back under moonlight
I watch the geese fly.

Roman Zoller (7)
John Ball Primary School, Blackheath

The Dragon

The wind passed by as the dragon flew by,
It soars through the air like a walking stare,
It flies up high to the sky, its wing is as huge as a giant's head,
And teeth as sharp as a sharp knife in the air,
You will only see him in his cave, lying on gold and laughing away.

A brave knight came who wandered through the dragon's cave,
The dragon roared but the knight was not going to flee,
He pulled out his sword and hit the dragon in the wing,
The dragon cried out in pain, shutting and covering his wing,
He felt pain like never before, he wanted to disappear like all the rest,
The knight ran to the castle telling the queen all he had seen.

Oduwa Evbuomwan (9)
Kentmere Academy And Nursery, Rochdale

Safari

One eye opens,
Then number two.
The day of our safari trip,
No, not the zoo!

We're all excited,
We fly out of bed,
Get ourselves ready,
Then get us all fed.

The bus arrives,
And we all pile on,
I'm at the front,
It's so much fun.

Ostrich and camels,
Rhinos and deer,
Lions and antelopes,
They're coming so near!

Then the time comes,
To see the baboons,
They're sat on the roof,
Acting like loons.

It's time to escape,
Back to the calm,
The bus has survived,
With no real harm.

Now to my favourite,
The sea lion show,
With Louis and Roger,
Who could say no?

All that is left,
For us to see,
Are the elephants and giraffes,
And the funfair - yippee!

Esta-Mae Hodgson (9)
Kentmere Academy And Nursery, Rochdale

Oh, Nature

Inspired by 'Nature Poem' by Bonnie Harding

Close your eyes and you can see
The way the world's supposed to be
Sun shining on a pale blue sky
While soft breezes pass by

Stars glaze throughout the night
To give you support, brightness and light
Trees grow as long as they can be
To give us oxygen and a reason to live

Grass grows for rich and poor
Proud and humble, high and low
Birds off in the distance
Blackbirds down below
Walking around the field
A solitary crow

Feel the wind in your hair
Smell the flowers bloom everywhere
See the beauty
Today is a new day
Enjoy nature, God's gift to you.

Lavinia Rosca (9)
Kentmere Academy And Nursery, Rochdale

The Boy Who Went Up To Space

A boy once lived in a small town on top of a very high cloud. His parents got into a fight on one terrible night. He went to the woods so afraid and alone and found a rocket ship and went into space. He found his new blue alien friends; they discovered a curse down below and checked it out with no worries at all. They realised what they did was a mistake and returned to the ship; they had found a cure to all this mayhem. They went back to Earth and played all day and night and had no problems and their smiles shone like a beautiful rainbow way up high. Later that night, they discussed returning to space and living their dreams high.

Ibrahim Martaza (9)
Kentmere Academy And Nursery, Rochdale

Halloween

Finally, this day comes around,
Where the air is filled with lots of sound.
Howling winds and cackling witches,
Skeletons and Frankensteins with stitches.

Pumpkins decorated all over town,
As people dress up as killer clowns.

Knock on doors and receive treats,
As children ask for more sweets.

When the Halloween day ends with a crash,
Everyone empties their buckets to see what is in their stash.

Kashif Hussain (9)
Kentmere Academy And Nursery, Rochdale

I Am A Girl And I Am Not Ashamed

Yes, I am a girl and I stand for my right,
Yes, I am a girl and I put up a fight,
I have a right to my education,
I have a right to play sports,
I have a right to play games,
I have a right to have fun,
I can run around the streets feeling nice and free,
Free from all the violence and free from all the poverty,
Football is my opportunity for my bright future ahead,
I am a girl and I am not ashamed, I said.

Peggy Jones (9)
Kentmere Academy And Nursery, Rochdale

My Name Is...

E is for energetic, cheerful and smiley
K is for kindness, you always show
A is for adventurous, always on the go
M is for marvellous, delightful to know
N is for nice, as kind as a sunset
O is for organised, happy to say
O is for optimistic, born to be attached
R is for relax, you know how.

Ekamnoor is much more than a name.

Ekamnoor Singh (9)
Kentmere Academy And Nursery, Rochdale

My Poem

Fast flier
Worm eater
Loud singer
Annoying talker
Multicoloured squawker
Air soaring diver
Sharp spotter
Insect swallower
Feather picker
Seed pecker
Naughty pooper
Mouse killer
Irritating tweeter
Cute looker
Small hunter
Water lover
Food provider
What am I?

Answer: A bird.

Musa Musaib (10)
Kentmere Academy And Nursery, Rochdale

Tigers

Majestic and strong with stripes along
I rule the land, my roar is grand
With night vision strong, I hunt before long
Though I love the fresh meat, it's not human I greet
Alone I walk in the silence
I stalk through the forest with ease
Beneath the tall trees.
Who am I?

Saad Khalid (9)
Kentmere Academy And Nursery, Rochdale

Nature's Song

N ature's wonders all around,
A s trees grow tall from the ground,
T rilling birds sing in the sky,
U nderneath the sun so high,
R ivers flow, both wild and free,
E arth's sweet gifts for you and me.

Dawud Raza (9)
Kentmere Academy And Nursery, Rochdale

Top Bins!

Saturday morning,
I wake up early
Get dressed in my kit
And my hair is all curly.

Eating my breakfast,
Drinking my juice
My mum got me Prime
To give me a boost.

Head down to the pitch,
Ready for the game.
My nickname is O-Dog
And I cannot be tamed.

Hoping for a win,
Not a lose, not a draw.
Straight into top bins!
My family saw me score!

Oscar Donlon (8)
Kidmore End CE Primary School, Kidmore End

Growing Up

G ather together to hear the story of the little girl who
was growing up,
R ight when you were five you made a new friend, you
both ate lollipops,
O h no! You hit double digits, in just a few more
minutes.
W ow, already eighteen, a young adult. Kids grow up
so fast,
I 'm so happy for you! Thirty-two years old already
getting married,
N o way! I'm going to be a grandmother, you've got
children! Nathaniel and Annie,
G rowing up is really difficult. Your children had more
children.

U m, I have so many grandchildren,
P hew, we're done, or are we? Your child asks, "What
was it like growing up?" Sigh, They're as annoying
as parrots.

Princess Mary Tazi Nsambu (9)
Our Lady & St Joseph RC Primary School, Hackney

Emotion Makes Us Cry Sometimes

Emotions make me happy.
Emotions make me sad.
Emotions make me human.
Emotions make me glad.
When I see injustice,
Emotions make me mad.
A feeling that is painful,
And makes my soul feel bad.
Everybody has them,
And everybody knows,
The feelings that we focus on,
Are surely set to grow.
So if you're feeling happy,
Be sure to smile and pray,
For giving thanks to God, our Father,
Adds blessings to our day.
But if you're feeling sad or lonely,
Never be dismayed,
As a prayer to God on these hard days,
Can chase the blues away.

The biggest feeling that we feel,
Is a special thing called love.
It's how I feel about my family and friends,
And how they feel about me.
Life can be tough, unfair and cruel,
So the way we feel may crash and fall.
We must hold our heads up high,
Proud, tall, with tears in our eyes through it all.
Emotions make us cry sometimes,
It is a reminder for us all.
So remember to love a lot,
Laugh a lot,
Live your life,
Because it is the only life we have got.

Sophia St Louis (9)
Our Lady & St Joseph RC Primary School, Hackney

Astro Cow

Hello, my name is Astro Cow,
I'm deep in outer space right now,
I'm off to visit distant stars
I've seen the moon, I've been to Mars,
I've done the most amazing things,
I've soared through Saturn's massive rings,
I have checked out Neptune and Pluto too,
Then out among the stars I flew,
I built this awesome rocket ship,
To take an interstellar trip,
And travel through the galaxy,
To find a home for cows like me,
You see, I used to live on Earth,
It was my home, my place of birth,
But now I search for somewhere new,
Somewhere they don't sell barbecues.
Astro Cow, Astro Cow, that's me, black and white,
I'm chewing cud all day and night,
I enjoy the journey in space and I eat cheese,
Milk, cream I give to you,
I want to live somewhere,
I don't smell meat,

And where people will say I'm cute,
Somewhere I could be the best,
And not the worst.

Narabi Vera Ilumoka (10)
Our Lady & St Joseph RC Primary School, Hackney

Friendship Is...

Friendship is like a rainbow,
So colourful and bright,
It's like a warm embrace,
That makes everything feel just right.

Friends are there to laugh with,
And wipe away your tears,
They're like a shining star,
Guiding you through your fears.

They share in all your joy,
And ease your lonely days,
With a friend by your side,
Life feels like a joyful maze.

So let's cherish our friends,
And hold them close and tight,
For in the journey of life,
They make everything feel just right.

Annalise Campbell (9)
Our Lady & St Joseph RC Primary School, Hackney

Haunted House

In the middle of the spooky woods,
There was a house with ghosts in bad moods,
Werewolves howled every full moon,
And zombies prowled through corridors in every room.

The house was big, black and dusty,
With a car in the garage that couldn't be more musty,
A garden as lifeless as a dead dinosaur,
And in the corner of the backyard, there was a
decaying dog paw.

A skeleton's bony fingers held his head up high,
So never even go to that mansion if you don't want to
die.

Eliott Arnoux (9)
Our Lady & St Joseph RC Primary School, Hackney

Feelings

Joy jumps and leaps,
Bright and bold,
Sorrow stands low,
Soft and cold.
Anger storms,
With thunder's roar.
Fear fog whispers,
At the door.
Love bright glows,
Warm and wide.
Guilt ghost hides,
Cannot abide.
Hope - horizon,
Is stunningly clear.
Each emotion,
Like a friend.
Guides us through,
The twists and bends.
In this world,
We laugh and cry,
Feelings dance,
Let us soar and fly,
Through rainbow skies.

Elijah McKenzie (10)
Our Lady & St Joseph RC Primary School, Hackney

We Stick Together Forever

Together we stick together
Together forever
We will surrender together
Whenever, forever we need each other
However, if a bear attacks
We always stick together, whatever
If we are high in the sky we will always be together
No matter what with each other
We will always be friends
Even if travelling 500 miles away from each other
In the future, we will grow old together
And travel the world, the whole entire planet.

Geralda Maria (9)
Our Lady & St Joseph RC Primary School, Hackney

Bea And Me Will Always Be

The first school that I went to
I met a girl called Bea
And when we started talking
We had a backstory

We discovered through our parents
We know this for a fact
Our great-grandfathers, Bill and Jack
Were quite the double act

Me and Bea would love to play
All day and the odd night
I miss not seeing her all the time
Bea's in my heart, but out of sight.

Ava Slaymaker
Our Lady & St Joseph RC Primary School, Hackney

Our Earth

There are eight planets,
That wear colourful jackets.
Vibrant blue, dusty red and mostly beige.
But people and animals live on one.

The sun keeps us warm,
Everywhere in any place,
The sun is so bright,
It blinds my sight.

This is our Earth,
And it's filled with mirth,
It's the place of my birth,
So let's look after our Earth.

Haviliah Ojarikre (9)
Our Lady & St Joseph RC Primary School, Hackney

Endless Potential

In a world of endless potential
It was filled with happiness and joy
There were animals and nature everywhere
And it was powered by the sun
Anything is possible
And you can be yourself
You can't stop getting better
You can be wherever you want to be
And whoever you want to be
Endless potential is a world of opportunity
Endless potential is happiness.

Luca Grossi (9)
Our Lady & St Joseph RC Primary School, Hackney

Nature's Gift

Haiku poetry

Fragile flowers bloom
Graceful butterflies flutter
Grass as soft as fur.

Elegant peacocks
Parade the beautiful lands
Like delicate webs.

Bees sipping nectar
From orchids so beautiful
Soon summer will come.

Green grasshoppers leap
From soft petal to petal
In this world of dew.

Ivy Neave (9)
Our Lady & St Joseph RC Primary School, Hackney

Animal Universe

A nimals are cute and they like to play the flute.
N ight animals are clever, even in bad weather.
I nsects can fly, but they are not a spy.
M ammals are animals, but some eat meat.
A lligators bite, so you shall not fight.
L ove your animals as you love yourself.

Niamh Buck (10)
Our Lady & St Joseph RC Primary School, Hackney

Heroes

H eroic helpers around the world,
E verything and everyone was kept safe,
R escuing hurt people as fast as a doctor's car,
O h! We need your help!
E very morning, every night, they are here to fight,
S o there's nowhere evil can even hide.

Aleks Leszkowicz (9)
Our Lady & St Joseph RC Primary School, Hackney

The Lunch

G ot to have it every day
A h how I love gammon
M y favourite food
M um tries to give me salmon
O nly I don't like fish!
N o, all I want is gammon!

Lois Dunn (9)
Our Lady & St Joseph RC Primary School, Hackney

Foxes Are Cute

F ox in a box was looking for its socks,
O wns the socks because it lives in a box,
X -ray the fox because it ate the socks!

Anya Piwowarek (9)
Our Lady & St Joseph RC Primary School, Hackney

Here Are Some Reasons

Here are some reasons
Why I love the seasons
Spring, it's almost the start of a new brain-boggling year (almost)
Where everyone likes to sing and cheer
It's spring, it's spring, my gosh it's here.

Summertime sun
Where it's too hot to run
Bathing in the light
Whilst the aeroplanes take flight.

Autumn starts getting chilly
And people start getting silly, because here comes Halloween
As I shuffle my feet through the leaves
And the crunch as they fall off the trees.

Winter choir singing outside by the door
Singing merrily to donate to the poor
Happy times, it's Christmas
People start making a wish list.

Those are my seasons.

Niamh Allen (11)
Priors Field Primary School, Kenilworth

Superb Seasons

As the crunchy leaves fall to the ground,
They do not make a single sound.
As the sun rises and falls,
The morning and evening calls.
Autumn.

Soft snow on the gritty pavement,
Not a time to camp in a tent.
Santa Claus comes to your house,
Creeping in and out like a mouse.
Winter.

At this time, flowers start to bloom,
Summertime will be here soon.
A gentle breeze runs through the sky,
I sometimes wonder why.
Spring.

The sun sets every single day,
But never ends in the same way.
So for this, I say hooray!
Summer.

Niamh R (10)
Priors Field Primary School, Kenilworth

The Magical Sleigh

I was sleeping one magical night
Reading with a very bright light
It was the middle of the night
And the moon was shining well tonight.

I heard the sound of jingling bells
And shouted for my mum to tell
I went outside to take a look
And saw someone reading a book.

I heard a banging on the roof
It sounded like a stamping hoof
I went inside to knead some dough
And heard Santa Claus, "Ho ho ho!"

Toby Shute (8)
Priors Field Primary School, Kenilworth

Seasons

As the snow slowly fades away,
And March rolls in,
I shout, "Hooray for spring"
But as spring draws to an end,
Summer starts, so let's play pretend.
Then as leaves start to fall,
I shout, "It's time for an autumn ball!"
But now it's colder,
And I'm getting older,
Winter is here to stay.

Jess B (10)
Priors Field Primary School, Kenilworth

Planets

Haiku poetry

Closest to the sun
Mercury's the smallest one
Venus is hotter

I'm the water one
I am an acid giant
Second from the sun

Humans live on Earth
I'm in the Goldilocks zone
Water is on Earth

I'm the red planet
I have two moons that will crack
I had lands and lakes.

Penny B (9)
Priors Field Primary School, Kenilworth

Halloween

It's Halloween,
And the ghosts move unseen,
As the cats prowl the street,
Looking for treats.
The pumpkins stare,
With a spooky glare,
And the children shout,
"Trick or treat!"
The wind moves the leaves,
Disturbing the trees,
The wolves howl,
And the cats meeeoowww.

Charlotte Williams (9)
Priors Field Primary School, Kenilworth

Footy Roger

Footy Roger loves to be a dodger
As dodging as he can be
But his daily routine went wrong
He got dressed but forgot to brush his teeth
So he got undressed
And brushed his teeth
And then cooked his breakfast
Then got dressed again
But by now
His breakfast was burnt.

Joseph Ballinger (9)
Priors Field Primary School, Kenilworth

Animal Party

Buzzy bees,
Mice eat cheese,
Hyenas laugh,
Giraffes are tall,
Jellyfish sting,
Killer whales swim,
Octopuses change colour,
Flamingos are pink,
Tortoises live for 100 years,
Kangaroos are jumping,
This is the animal party.

Winnie CW (8)
Priors Field Primary School, Kenilworth

Space

Dogs on Mars, in the spa
The sun eats a bun
Space and ace
Soon moon
But you moon salute
The one at the top of the tree
Is the planet of Eek
I'm Mercury the smallest
Of them all.

Evie Whiter (7)
Priors Field Primary School, Kenilworth

Spectacular Space

Planet Mars is where you find stars
Planet Earth is where you give birth
Planets Ceres and Eris are dwarf planets
In different space belts
Their existence is felt.

Mabel Folliot (9)
Priors Field Primary School, Kenilworth

Moon, Soon And Noon

I will go to the moon,
And I promise to come back soon.
But I can only come back in the noon...
Hello dear, I got back from the moon.

Maysa Ma (8)
Priors Field Primary School, Kenilworth

The Twin Comedy Show

Based on 'The Land Of Roar'

P ow I go but you don't know
R oar is where I live but you don't know so good luck
O h and I might be as pale as a vampire
S ome day I will see my mate
E asy but you wouldn't say that
C ome, I have some hair
C ome, but not too close if you come
O n and over the moon

Who am I?

Will I be magical?
In Roar, I am crazy-mad
No one can be as wise as I
In Roar, I have lived in a place there
No, I might have travelled somewhere?
Jam is red but I have sweets of jelly beans and butterscotch
Am I who you think?
Who am I?

Jack Hopstein (8)
St Anne's CE Primary School, Godmanchester

The Winged Flying Machine

I have eyes like glowing amber gems,
I can obliterate mountains with a *whoosh!* a *bang!* and a *sizzle*!
My scales radiate a shade of red like a wildfire,
My teeth glint in the sunlight like daggers,
I can fly but I'm not a falcon.
What am I?

We can frighten the life out of you and give you a heart attack,
We can drain you and turn you into one of us,
We have eyes like black holes in a night sky,
We have stitches holding us together,
What are we?

James Cashman (8)
St Anne's CE Primary School, Godmanchester

Riddled Land Of Roar

I have a nest but I'm not a crow, raven or a bird,
I have an army but I'm not military or police,
I might make you sneeze or be frightened,
I come out at night but I'm not a bat,
I capture people but I'm not a kidnapper.
Who am I?

I have powers like a witch but I'm not,
I do have great power over spells,
I want to catch someone but not like the police or FBI,
I have great sneaking skills but I'm not a ninja,
I have friends,
Who am I?

Jilord Churchill (8)
St Anne's CE Primary School, Godmanchester

The Twin Fantasy

I have mechanical eyes that stare right through you
but I'm not a robot,
I am like the night sky full of stars but I'm not space,
I rock like a cot but I'm not a bed,
I come alive but I'm not in your world,
What am I?

I have amazing amber wings but I'm not a bird,
I can fly but not in your land,
I have fire in my throat but I'm not stacks of wood,
I've got deep brown eyes,
I heat up but I'm not an oven or microwave,
What am I?

Nina Zolnowska (8)
St Anne's CE Primary School, Godmanchester

What Am I?

I am not used but I'm not a web,
I am impossible to fold but I'm not wood,
Arthur weed in it but I'm not a toilet,
I am a portal but I am not a plane.
What am I?

I have got calm, swaying water, but I'm not a pool,
My water is as cold as ice, but it is not Antarctica,
The rocks are as sharp as blades but I'm not a knife,
I come from the scary bad side, but I'm not a tangled forest.
What am I?

Answer: The land of Roar!

Freddie Mews (9)
St Anne's CE Primary School, Godmanchester

Poem Of Beauty

My wings are as slight as string but I'm not a bat
My scales are rainbow-coloured, but I'm not a fish
I might give you a ride, but I'm not a Pegasus
I eat meat but I'm not an animal in your world
What am I?

I'm a cheetah when I run, but I'm not one
I have a sword, but I'm not a knight
I have a cloak, but I'm not a scientist
I jump, but I'm not a frog
What am I?

Caden Outridge
St Anne's CE Primary School, Godmanchester

The Land Of Roar

I blow fire but I'm not a flame-thrower
I fly around but I'm not a bird
I'm a living creature but not in this world
I have eyes like marble
I have deadly rays but I'm not the sun
What am I?
I have a nest but I'm not a bird
I rule my land but I'm not a king
I'm darker than the night but I'm not a crow
I go out at night but I'm not a hedgehog
What am I?

Harrison Bishop (8)
St Anne's CE Primary School, Godmanchester

Roar

I have a sneaky army, but I'm not a soldier,
I'm a villain, but not one you have heard of,
I live in a nest but I'm not a bird,
I will suck away energy but I'm not a drain,
What am I?

I have blue hair but I'm not a doll,
My house is on an island but I'm not alone,
I do spells but I'm not a wizard,
My scales are teal but I'm not a fish,
What am I?

Autumn Shortt (9)
St Anne's CE Primary School, Godmanchester

The Twin Riddley, The Land Of Roar

I have blue hair like a human
But I'm not a Barbie doll
I have a turquoise tail
But I'm not a turtle
I have a spell book
But I'm not a wizard
I live in the ocean
But you can't see me
What am I?

I'm orange, but not a fire
I fly, but I'm not a bird
I breathe fine, but I'm not the sun
I help people, but I'm not a human
Who am I?

Aoife Yetton (8)
St Anne's CE Primary School, Godmanchester

The Land Of Roar Creatures

I have shiny scales, but I am not a dragon
I have blueish hair, but I am not a woman who died her hair
I have magical powers, but I am not a witch
I am a combination of half and half, but I'm not an animal
Who am I?

I have feathers, but I'm not a bird
I have straw, but I'm not a scarecrow
I'm half and half, but still a creature
I stand on one foot
Who am I?

Gloria Leacock (8)
St Anne's CE Primary School, Godmanchester

Lovely Land Of Roar

I have a sewn-up mouth, but I am not a puppet
I have terrifying balls of fire raging out of my sockets, but I am not a dragon
I like furries but I am not a monster
What am I?

I have shimmering teal, pearl-coloured scales, but I am not a fish
I have blue curly hair like the ocean, but I am not a Barbie
I hold powers in my palms, but I am not a wizard
What am I?

Ava Stoehr (8)
St Anne's CE Primary School, Godmanchester

Land Of Roar

I have bright red scales.
They shine in the sun.
I am like a flying blow torch.
My eyes are neon-green.
I'm sometimes as aggressive as a lion.
What am I?

My turquoise scales shine like pearls.
I have sapphire-blue curly hair.
I am like a swimming fish.
I have magical powers but I'm not a wizard.
Who am I?

Edward Risley-Settle (8)
St Anne's CE Primary School, Godmanchester

In The Magical Land

I have an army with a military chief
I'm at war but not in your world
I need to take over the land as vicious as I am
I'm not a demon
What am I?

I can fly but I'm not a bird
I can roar but I'm not a dinosaur
I'm ambitious but I'm not a murderer
I produce smoke but I'm not fire
What am I?

Jeremiah Smith (9)
St Anne's CE Primary School, Godmanchester

The Land Of Roar

I have pearls and I am not a fish that lives in the sea.
I have a tail but I am not a dog.
I have scales but I am not a catfish.
I have magical spells but I am not a wizard.
I have beautiful hair just like diamonds in the sky.
I have bright hair.
I will kill you.
I am scary.
I have amazing skills.
What am I?

Mufaro Precious Nyakuedzwa (8)
St Anne's CE Primary School, Godmanchester

What Am I?

I have crystal-blue hair like the ocean,
I have scales but I'm not a fish,
I can do spells like a wizard,
I love the water but I don't drink it,
What am I?

I fly in the sky but I'm not a bug,
I breathe fire,
I'm big and scary,
I eat small things,
What am?

Sienna Price (9)
St Anne's CE Primary School, Godmanchester

Riddle Land Of Roar

I'm really good at kung fu but I am not a ninja
I have a head but I am not a human,
I might beat you up but I could also do a spell on you,
I hide in a cave but I am not a bat,
I am trying to catch someone but I am not Spider-Man,
I have a friend that lives with a grandad.

Who am I?

Leonardo Wright (8)
St Anne's CE Primary School, Godmanchester

Upon The Water

I have crystal-blue hair
I live on a rock in deep sea
My tail is full of blue scales
Magnificent blue ocean.
Who am I?

I have brown hair with a slight shimmer
I'm covered in glitter.
In some places I come to life
Mechanical eyes, silver and glittery.
What am I?

Lilah Pennington (9)
St Anne's CE Primary School, Godmanchester

Evil Times

I sound like a bird
And I have a yellow beak
I look like a bird
I'm as deadly as a lion
I have colossal wings
And I have lots of eyes
I have a dungeon
I'm as big as Godzilla
I got you, I am quick
I have a mighty castle
I have an army
What am I?

Oscar Hooper (8)
St Anne's CE Primary School, Godmanchester

Pickle

Based on 'The Land of Roar'

One day Pickle was in Grandad's attic at night
When Pickle was in there she had her eyes glued to the spooky window.
One day Pickle suddenly jumped into the attic.
Rose told Arthur that he was starting to get bored.
Pickle did not like Arthur because Rose said he was not very nice.

Thomas Hepworth (8)
St Anne's CE Primary School, Godmanchester

What Am I?

I have horns but I'm not a cow
My tail is foul
I have golden wings but I'm not a bird
And I don't like herbs.

I'm a house for some
I gloss and glisten in the sun
I'm fun for counting, one, two, three
And like a mountain.

Fynn Rowland (8)
St Anne's CE Primary School, Godmanchester

The Entrance To Roar

I am the entrance to a land,
Not a wardrobe, you see,
I live next to Prosecco in an attic,
I was a snake that swallowed a pig
When Grandad got stuck in me,
I look like somebody weed on me,
Rose isn't interested in me.
What am I?

Hartley Jackson (8)
St Anne's CE Primary School, Godmanchester

The Land Of Roar

I have pink glittery hair, but I'm not a Barbie doll.
I have purple, shimmering, pearly scales, but I'm not a fish.
I have a tail that sparkles in the sun, but I'm not a dragon.
I live in the ocean but not in your world,
Who am I?

Samantha Ogeh (8)
St Anne's CE Primary School, Godmanchester

Evil Lifetime

I kill new animals, I am as powerful as a jaguar,
I have a shock of lightning when I talk,
I am a wave crashing with anger,
I am as evil as a poisonous snake,
I am a black-coated dragon with razor-sharp teeth.
What am I?

Millie Gilbert (8)
St Anne's CE Primary School, Godmanchester

The Land Of Roar

I rock, but I'm not a rock band.
I have a black, pearl, glittery sparkle, but I'm not a sticker.
I have legs, but I cannot run.
I have eyes like the ocean, but I'm not a merman or mermaid.
What am I?

Alexander Akinyele (8)
St Anne's CE Primary School, Godmanchester

Untitled

I have wings but I'm not a bird
I've got button eyes but I'm not a doll
I have a big army but I'm not a soldier
I like to squeeze but I'm not a snake
Do you know who I am?

Nora Webb (9)
St Anne's CE Primary School, Godmanchester

What Am I?

I have powers but I am not a superhero.
I have a cape like the night sky but I am not Superman.
I have a hat shaped like a conical mountain but I am not a mountain.

What am I?

Hayden Warren-Rea (8)
St Anne's CE Primary School, Godmanchester

Space Is A Good Place

Hello, this is about space,
And it's going to be ace.
And we're going to an amazing place.
Mercury has days which last twice as long as a year,
And it's one of the planets that's shaped perfectly like a sphere.

Venus is the only planet in our solar system that spins backwards relative to the other planets,
And on Earth, there are lots of bunny rabbits.
The sun is 400 times the size of the moon,
And by the time you fly to space, it will be past noon.

Our sun is only considered to be an average-sized star,
Now let's fly to the sun, but it is very far.
The sun's mass takes up 99.86 percent of the group of our entire solar system,
In space, you have got lots of freedom.

Neptune has days sixteen hours long,
And the atmosphere is really strong.
Thanks for listening, by the way, space is amazing.

Sofia Jackson (9)
St Monica's RC Primary School, Flixton

The Competition

Today is the day of the competition.
I am in a fright, but my emotion is still bright.
I put on my leotard and my mum does my hair,
I must look perfect for the judges, they really care.
We hop in the car, we don't live very far.
Ten minutes later and we are halfway there.
I am so nervous, we have arrived and I register at the desk, I eagerly wait.
It is me, they call out my name.
My mum and dad cheer, they make me have no fear.
I present to the judges, my moves need to be bold to win the gold.
I begin my routine, everything is going like a dream.
Spinning through the air doing what I love, I can see everybody looking at me from above.
Now for the hardest trick.
I have landed it, the crowd are in shock because I rock.
They applaud and I finish with a gleaming smile.
After my routine I have to wait a little while.
I am nervous, my palms are sweating.
They call out third place and it goes to my friend.
Second place goes to another competitor, we always contend.
It is time.

First place is announced, it is me! I prance to the stage to receive my trophy.
Shiny and gold, I am so proud to hold.
I can't wait to go home, to tell my brother Tommy.

Emilia Attwood (9)
St Monica's RC Primary School, Flixton

Friendship Forever

Once upon a poem, there lived two friends. They always had a dream, and that dream was to go to space. One day, they asked their mums when they were both ten, and they said yes and they cheered with glee and danced around the room. They packed their bags and built a rocket and zoomed into space with each other. They were as fast as cheetahs!
Boom! Then they realised they hit the moon and they timidly poked their two little heads out of the door to see where they were going to explore in space.
One of them said, "Wow! Space looks as magical as magic."
Then they both said, "Let's see what to explore."
They saw moon rocks, they saw holes in the moon.
One of them said, "Space is as dreamy as a dream. I'm serious!"
Then they both agreed they should go home and have some hot chocolate. They were best friends forever.

Yasmin McKenna (7)
St Monica's RC Primary School, Flixton

My Emotions

Today I'm feeling angry,
It makes me want to shout,
And stomp and wear my mean face,
To let my anger out,
Instead of using my words,
To say what I'm mad about.

Today I feel sad,
It makes me want to cry,
I pout my lips,
I whine and whimper and sniffle, sob and sigh,
Instead of using my words,
To tell everybody why.

Today I'm feeling happy,
It makes me want to run,
I go wild and act all crazy,
Until the day is done,
Instead of using my words,
So that we can all have good fun.

Today my feelings get too strong,
And I know it's time to say,
So I use my words to show how I feel,
In a safe and healthy way.

Mikey Gallager (8)
St Monica's RC Primary School, Flixton

Geography

G eography is my favourite subject.
E xciting Egyptian pyramids stand proud in Cairo.
O ceans surround the seven continents of the Earth.
G lorious Great Britain is bustling with exciting places
to visit.
R ome, the capital of Italy, is home to the Pope.
A ntarctica is the coldest place on Earth.
P icturesque Paris, the heart of the 2024 Olympics.
H igh-speed bullet trains whizz through Japan.
Y ou're never too old to explore the world!

Michael Nesbitt (8)
St Monica's RC Primary School, Flixton

My Little Bird's Day

Beautiful bird flying high
Swooping, soaring in the sky
You make me smile, all day long
I love to listen to your sweet song
You have big, blue, beady eyes
And colourful feathers, my, oh my
You gather twigs to make your nest
Oh poor little thing, you must need a rest
You eat your worms, can't get enough
In your tree as I look above
It is night-time now so lay down your head
The moon is bright, it is time for bed.

Jasmine Smith (7)
St Monica's RC Primary School, Flixton

My Cat... Coco

Coco goes on his perch,
Sleeping, daydreaming,
And purring.
He thinks about,
All the birds, butterflies and bees,
And how he chases them,
Round the garden.

He wakes up stirring,
With an empty tummy.
On the hunt for breakfast and dinner.
Coco sleeps with Pumpkin,
Curled up together,
And it's so cute.
Pumpkin fights with Coco,
All the time,
About the cat tree.

Aibhlinn Maguire (7)
St Monica's RC Primary School, Flixton

In Space, I Saw

In space, I saw a galaxy,
As purple as a grape.
I looked up and saw stars twinkling in the night sky,
With rockets zooming past which caught my eye.
Planets of every shape and size,
Some too big for my eyes.
Some planets have many moons, Earth has only one,
Some have none.
You can fly into space using a white rocket,
To explore the world above us.

Jessica Kelly (7)
St Monica's RC Primary School, Flixton

Untitled

Roses are red, violets are blue,
They're on the planet and we need to protect it too.

We have one Earth.
If we don't put in our heart, we can't rebuild.
We can't make it if it happens
We will be floating in space.

Plant a tree, stop poaching
Let them be free.
The Earth is ours which we protect
Let's save it for the rest.

Ifechi Etolue (8)
St Monica's RC Primary School, Flixton

The Wicked Witch

Did you know there was a mean witch called Twitch?
And she liked to play on a pitch.

Well, not every witch is mean but,
This one is the meanest witch ever!
She almost put me in a potion,
But luckily my friend saved me from that awful witch!
She even called me a rat,
But I called her a bat.

Emily Morris (7)
St Monica's RC Primary School, Flixton

I Love Nature

Green grass, blue skies
All the tiny insects
The fluttering butterflies

The rivers, lakes and water
The branches and the logs
The snails, the slugs and the fishes
And the slimy green frogs

Nature is amazing
Forests, full of trees
Flowers, colourful just like bumblebees.

Fionn Whiting (7)
St Monica's RC Primary School, Flixton

A Winter's Day

Foxes running across the frosty grass,
People wearing warm woolly hats.
When it is cold I wear earmuffs and drink hot chocolate,
Friends go skating on slippery surfaces,
Families sit together on the 25th of December.

Penny Petrou (9)
St Monica's RC Primary School, Flixton

All About Animals

All about animals like tigers
A tiger's child is called a cub
An average adult tiger can grow to about 96 centimetres.

A squid can weigh between 300 grams and 500 grams
When it's fully grown.

Madeline Yuille (8)
St Monica's RC Primary School, Flixton

Dragons

D ragons are fierce and dangerous,
R oaring like thunder.
A mazingly cool and loud,
G reat big wings,
O utstandingly big and brave,
N ever seen but always believed.

Caleb Fitzgerald (7)
St Monica's RC Primary School, Flixton

Friendship

F orever nice
R eally relaxed
I ncredible
E xciting
N ever let you down
D on't laugh when things go wrong
S uper funny

Friends forever!

Ivy Whitworth (8)
St Monica's RC Primary School, Flixton

My Family

My family is always by my side
I couldn't love them more if I tried
I love my family so much,
I just love to give them a cwtch.

Ava Whitworth (7)
St Monica's RC Primary School, Flixton

Spring

A haiku

Splash! Drip! Rain falls down,
Lambs are born, white as snowdrops,
Flowers start to bloom.

Evelina Dorling (10)
St Monica's RC Primary School, Flixton

Animals And The Haunted House

There was a little cat. The little cat was called Bella. And there was a dog. The dog was called Lilly.
Bella and Lilly went to the haunted house. In the haunted house there was a spell book. In the spell book it said 'This is a spell book with lots of different spells'.
In the book there was magic. The house was dark. Then Lilly and Bella were scared. Lilly and Bella hid because a light came on. Then the light started to flash.
Lilly and Bella ran away. They ran out of the door because they were scared.
They left the haunted house and they never went back to the haunted house again.
Bella and Lilly were scared all night.

Abbi Condie (9)
Stoneyburn Primary School, Bathgate

Christmas

C andles are on and shimmering.
H ats and scarves are on to keep you warm at night.
R ight at the fireplace nice and cosy.
I gloos are built with glistening snow.
S now is falling all around and
T here are sledges everywhere.
M ax is my dog with reindeer horns.
A t the little cabin happy as can be with my mum
watching TV.
S anta Claus is in town with all the presents in the
world.

Ava Lee (10)
Stoneyburn Primary School, Bathgate

The Man On The Moon

The man on the moon
He sings such a tune
Soon it is June
It is noon
And have to go soon
But he doesn't want to leave
His spoon on the moon
So he eats a prune
On the moon
With his spoon
And he jumps
In the goon
On the moon
With his spoon
And a prune
And he storms in his room
On the moon.

Lori Bryce (9)
Stoneyburn Primary School, Bathgate

My Emotions

E motions are okay to have.
M ad, angry and annoyed.
O n some days you might have bad days.
T imes you might have are okay.
I t's okay to be happy, mad and sad.
O n days you can feel everything.
N o one can just have happy days.
S ometimes I can feel bad.

Hollie Moore (8)
Stoneyburn Primary School, Bathgate

Cool Space!

S pace is a special place to be.
P laces in space are so magical, you wouldn't believe it.
A mazing things to see in space.
C ool, magical rocks to be collected.
E xcited when you pass the colourful galaxy.

Leah O'Malley (10)
Stoneyburn Primary School, Bathgate

Animal Riddle

You can see me in Scandinavia and Alaska,
I'm a wild animal, not a pet.
I'm very tall, brown, and white all over,
I always help St Nick on the 25th.
What am I?

Answer: I am a reindeer.

Chloe Gilfether (10)
Stoneyburn Primary School, Bathgate

Winter

W ind
I cicle
N ice cosy nights
T ime to make hot chocolate
E normous presents
R eady or not, winter will come, get cosy or not.

Cora Pacey (9)
Stoneyburn Primary School, Bathgate

Believe In Yourself

If we all tried, gave, trusted and loved a little more,
The world would shine so beautifully,
Like it never has before,
If you're doing the best you can,
That's all you can do,
Just stay strong, have faith and perspective,
Until the world catches up to you.

Aroush Fatima Qasim (11)
Stopsley High School, Luton

Elemental Creatures

In a place made of stone,
A place where elements are shown,
Foxes of fire roaming free,
Small sparks turn into bees,
Teardrops of water are small little mice,
Majestic unicorns made of ice,
Puffy little clouds, baby birds learning to fly,
And small bits of soil, dragons with blue eyes,
Some will burn, some will freeze,
Others will let out a cool breeze,
So do not hurt these,
Beautiful creatures made of fire,
And water and earth and air,
Their amounts aren't getting higher.

Milly Stoker (10)
Terrington CE (VA) Primary School, Terrington

Nature

Nature is a forest,
Nature is a shade of green,
Nature is all around us, waiting to be seen.
Nature is the place we are destroying,
Nature is the place we are enjoying.
Nature can be annoying.
Nature has weeds and slugs,
Climbing throughout our woods.
Nature is becoming polluted,
The solutions are convoluted.
We have made this mess,
We have not done our best.
Nature is going and saying its last goodbye,
It will be gone unless we try,
So protect our nature!

Bea Tyreman (9)
Terrington CE (VA) Primary School, Terrington

Halloween

Pumpkins are full of light,
Brightens up the darkest night,
Spooks and scares, ghosts galore,
Coming to knock on your door,
Cobwebs and masks, spiders and bats,
Witches with their black pointy hats,
Witches and ghosts on the streets,
Coming to say, "Trick or treat!"
But we ate all the sweets!

Poppy Pesterfeild (10)
Terrington CE (VA) Primary School, Terrington

Sheep And Cows

S oft and cuddly
H ard to hear
E asily scared
E nergetic animal
P reparing for its predators.

C ows can fight a lot
O ut all over the field
W hen it rains they like to fight.

Matthew Whitcher (10)
Terrington CE (VA) Primary School, Terrington

Imagination

Thoughts inside your head
Lying in bed
Magic is here
Letting out a joyful tear.

Lost in my mind
All my bad thoughts are left behind
Magical things you might find
My thoughts are so kind.

Isabella Sharp (10)
Terrington CE (VA) Primary School, Terrington

Reptilian

R are and elusive reptiles roam around the hot and cold places all over the Earth.
E nergetic animals wander the world, collecting prey or plants, and avoiding predators.
P retty, patient reptiles, alive, slithering, crawling, finding their type.
T iny talented hunters, striking and biting till their prey stops the fight.
I ntelligent iguanas finding insects to ingest.
L ittle or large, we bask under the sun, using UVB because of our cold blood.
I nvasive, we wander far from our homes.
A doptable and adorable animals await a loving home to call their own.
N avigating narrow swamps at night is a piece of cake for an animal with such might.

Sasha Sefton (9)
Werrington Community Primary School, Yeolmbridge

The Weather

Silky hair fell down my face,
As the rain trickled out of the soft clouds,
Clouds filled the air, making it cold and dark,
Lightning lit up the sky as a tear fell down my face,
Boom!
Came the thunder, as I fell to the slippery ground,
My tears collided with the rain.

The rain slowed down,
The rain stopped.
Everything turned into a wonderland,
It was like nothing happened,
I don't think it did,

Said the witch, "Oh yes it did!"

Edie Short (9)
Whitchurch Primary School, Whitchurch

Wonderland

Wonderland is a cuckoo land where everything is crazy.
Wonderland is ruled by a bonkers queen.
Why oh why is she so mean?
She cuts off heads to make people dead.
"Enough of the queen," the Mad Hatter thought.
"We shall paint her roses green."
"She'll cut off my head but I'll cut off hers."
"We will all be safe."
"I'll kidnap her with my wondrous tarts."
Wonderland is a cuckoo land where everything is crazy.

Daisy Howell (10)
Whitchurch Primary School, Whitchurch

Lifeless Space

I find myself all alone,
Alone amidst the stars,
No food, water and no cars,
I searched to find any life,
Suddenly a hostile alien emerged,
But I had no choice but to kick it off,
Into the endless void, it fell.
I waved farewell.
But I heard a voice,
Watch your back, it phlegmed.
Your rocket is done, it phlegmed even more.
It then fell into the void,
No more from the alien,
something about my rocket,
it said...

Cole Preen (10)
Whitchurch Primary School, Whitchurch

Growing Up

When you're a baby, you're as smart as an ant.
When you're a toddler, you could crawl like a ladybird slowly and calmly.
When you're a child, you run wildly and freely like a cheetah.
When you're a teenager, you become slow like a sloth and have an attitude of a cat.
When you're an adult, you become tired and stressed like a koala.
When you're a senior, you become old and sad like a walrus.

Nell Smith (9)
Whitchurch Primary School, Whitchurch

Wonderverse

W atching
O bediently
N ow
D enying
E ven
R ougher
V oices
E cho
R aining
S adly
E nding

This poem is about this book,
You might be reading it in a cosy nook.
Never give up on your dream of writing,
But never let your guard down,
The ogre is coming from behind you!!

Chloe Page (9)
Whitchurch Primary School, Whitchurch

Your Imagination

In a wonderland far, far away
Whatever you think is there.
Beautiful birds flapping around,
A man fighting to the death, man vs griffin
Wonder slides taking you wherever you want
Parkour waiting to be done,
Games, cats, dogs,
Whatever you think or want is there before your eyes
But every story comes to an end
As you drift back home.

Leo Edwards
Whitchurch Primary School, Whitchurch

You Need To Be Careful Who You Are Friends With

It can be hard when you have to end a friendship.
This might help.
Stay with them but,
Slowly float away like a balloon and try to find other friends.
When going, you might find one worth a million.
If they try to make you come back,
But you don't want to,
Remember,
If you read a book twice it has the same ending.

Eloise Latham (9)
Whitchurch Primary School, Whitchurch

Emotions

People will always have different emotions.
My happy dreams fill the air with people shouting with delight.
People love and enjoy the dreams.

One person in the world is crying,
But two people help them and make her happy.

People always have different emotions,
But no matter what,
People will always help.

Hollie Williams (9)
Whitchurch Primary School, Whitchurch

The Enchanted Forest

Deep down in the enchanted forest,
Rough trees danced in the breeze,
And feathers drifted down from the sky.
The river covered the fairies as they swooped by,
And the unicorns galloped over the bridge.
But what the unicorns didn't know was that,
If you cross the bridge,
You can't escape the new world...

Gabija Ciunelis (10)
Whitchurch Primary School, Whitchurch

Space Is Wonder

Space is a place,
Space is spacious,
Anything could you paste,
Some planets are big, others are small,
They could be all sizes,
Whirpools whirl,
Whirpools suck,
Astronauts fly,
Astronauts land,
Astronauts can do anything,
Stars are bright,
Space is dark,
Space goes on forever.

Thomas Webley (9)
Whitchurch Primary School, Whitchurch

What Am I?

The hot chocolate looked me in the eyes.
What am I?
If I am not liked, I go into a deep, dark cave.
The hot chocolate looked me in the eyes.
What am I?
If I am too cold I am not liked but I'm too warm.
I am a safety hazard.
The hot chocolate looked me in the eyes.
What am I?

Charlie Young (9)
Whitchurch Primary School, Whitchurch

The Lion

Once upon a time, there was a lion.
He was as tanned as an orange.
The lion's teeth were as white as a white bone.
His mane was as fluffy as a fluffy teddy bear.
All lions are fluffy and cute,
Just imagine if you have a cat,
It is in the same family as a lion.

Vinny Skinner (9)
Whitchurch Primary School, Whitchurch

The Butterflies

B eautiful, special creatures,
U nique pictures,
T wirling,
T wilights,
E vil lights,
R ushy sights,
F iery nights,
L ies,
I scream,
E yes wide,
S inging brides.

Chantai Joseph (9)
Whitchurch Primary School, Whitchurch

What Is It?

Goes in water
Like crabs
That wear rags

Eats urchins
That are searching
For people's feet to stab

They hold hands
When they float
In coats
On a boat
What is it?

Answer: It's an otter.

Emily Alexander (9)
Whitchurch Primary School, Whitchurch

Friendship

Friendship is when people are friends,
Like your girls used to be,
Which is now no longer true.
Be careful with who you are friends with,
You might regret your choice of being friends,
With people you think are nice.
Remember to choose smartly.

Amelia Reeves (10)
Whitchurch Primary School, Whitchurch

Mental Health

Mental health, a phase you go through
Mental health, a place you go to
Mental health, a key you need
Mental health, a place you're free
Mental health, a bond between
Mental health, a place for your heart, for family and friends.

Scarlett Hill (10)
Whitchurch Primary School, Whitchurch

Who Is He?

He's as big as a dinosaur.
He's as brave and strong as a lion.
He's as kind as a god.
He's as clever as a teacher.
He's as green as an emerald when he is angry.
He always saves the day!
He is The Hulk.

Lawson-John Mullins-Rothwell (10)
Whitchurch Primary School, Whitchurch

Doggies

D oing crazy stuff,
O range dogs are amazing,
G oing to the park is fun,
G etting the rubber ball the human throws
I nto the bush,
E ating nibbles in a full bowl,
S o delicious!

Isabella Britton (9)
Whitchurch Primary School, Whitchurch

What's The Animal?

It's as sneaky as a mouse
The females are in charge
It likes to sunbathe
It has slinky fights
It is endangered
Some of them have rings on their tails
What are they?

Answer: Lemurs.

Esme Greenan (9)
Whitchurch Primary School, Whitchurch

My Imagination

I
M ove
A nimals
G ently
I n
N ature
A nd
T igers
I n
O nesies
N od.

Sophie Tovey (10)
Whitchurch Primary School, Whitchurch

Dreams Or Nightmares

Dream of pumpkins
Dream of muffins
Dream of little munchkins
Dream of zombies
But here come the nightmares
Nightmares of children
Nightmares of dreams.

Lily James (9)
Whitchurch Primary School, Whitchurch

What Am I?

I am everywhere, yet I am nowhere,
I travel the world, yet I'm in one place,
I howl in people's faces,
Yet I'm nowhere near them...
What am I?

Finley Knight (9)
Whitchurch Primary School, Whitchurch

Pandas

P erfect and fantastic
A nimals like pandas are
N aturally amazing
D oing
A stonishing
S tuff.

Meyra Mitkova (9)
Whitchurch Primary School, Whitchurch

I Shake

Shaking, relaxing
Relaxing, shaking
Calming my body
My thoughts
And my brain

Starlights shining, music ringing

As it creeps upon me
Eating me whole
I want to lie down
Forget all I know

Arms squeezing, bells dinging

For those five minutes
I lie on my back
Shaking my body
My brain is relaxed

Starlights shining, music ringing

As it creeps upon me
Eating me whole
I want to lie down
Forget all I know

Arms squeezing, bells dinging

For those five minutes
I lie on my back
Shaking my body
My brain is relaxed

Starlights shining, music ringing

As I shake
It slips away
Leaving me calm
Today

Arms squeezing, bells dinging
Starlights shining, music ringing.

Margot Mansfield Steinhäuser (10)
Wilbraham Primary School, Fallowfield

Wonderland

Wonderland is Wonderland but you don't think you can be wonderful too?
Well...
There is no need to see what you seek;
Just be what you want to be,
Because you should have the right to be free.
You feel you have the need but your needs don't lead to what you want to be.
The outside world is not what it seems,
To me, it's sunny and warm but sometimes you can get buried beneath the trees,
So just take a rest and you will see, you can be whatever you want to be,
From Wonderland to Wonderland, escape your dream and believe what you want to believe.

India Rose Denny (10)
Wilbraham Primary School, Fallowfield

Wonder

Do you ever wonder about a life
Without pain?
Or how many steps you take each
Single time.
Ever wonder where you wish to get
Away from those who
Hurt you!
Even if they apologise.
Did you ever wonder that the things
You do are a bad influence
As a role model.
Ever wonder what wonder is?
Have you wondered what confidence
Gives to children?
I guarantee that we wonder different
Things.
And that's unique.

Jumana Jabir (10)
Wilbraham Primary School, Fallowfield

Friends Forever

We are together forever and forever together
No matter how hard you try to separate us
We are like dandelions floating through the air
Almost as if time stops when we are together.

She is like my universe and I'm her galaxy
We need each other to work right
Like a high-five
But sometimes she has other stars
And I have other planets
But it's okay
Because we will always be the troublesome two.

Rayana Albadawi (10)
Wilbraham Primary School, Fallowfield

The Environment

I love nature and I know you do
But have you thought about plastic pollution?
Spreading everywhere
From down below
To up high
Plastic everywhere!

Olah Ahmed (10)
Wilbraham Primary School, Fallowfield

Spring

Beautiful plants glowing,
With their leaves growing.
Lots of colours around,
With the snow going.

Baby birds hatching,
As flowers begin to bloom.
The smell of spring is all around,
As sunshine fills the room.

In spring, Easter is celebrated,
Chocolate eggs are yummy sweets.
The Easter bunny hopping,
Children gathering treats.

As spring leaves, summer arrives,
Bunnies in the fields, like kangaroos hopping,
Seeds growing into tasty fruit,
Little strawberries you can't eat without stopping.

Violet Sheehy (10)
Ysgol Gynradd Gymunedol Gymraeg Llantrisant, Miskin

Halloween

It's almost Halloween.
I feel terrified.
I'm under my duvet.
Trying to hide.

The spooky day is here.
I need a mask, fast.
Beetlejuice will bring fear.
It's going to be a blast.

I go door to door, "Trick or treat?"
With my friends, collecting sweets.
They dare not give a treat or two.
Or we'll unleash the peek-a-boo!

Gwion Davies (11)
Ysgol Gynradd Gymunedol Gymraeg Llantrisant, Miskin

YOUNG WRITERS INFORMATION

We hope you have enjoyed reading this book – and that you will continue to in the coming years.

If you're the parent or family member of an enthusiastic poet or story writer, do visit our website **www.youngwriters.co.uk/subscribe** and sign up to receive news, competitions, writing challenges and tips, activities and much, much more! There's lots to keep budding writers motivated!

If you would like to order further copies of this book, or any of our other titles, then please give us a call or order via your online account.

Young Writers
Remus House
Coltsfoot Drive
Peterborough
PE2 9BF
(01733) 890066
info@youngwriters.co.uk

Join in the conversation!
Tips, news, giveaways and much more!

YoungWritersUK YoungWritersCW

youngwriterscw youngwriterscw